SATURDAY NIGHT

SATURDAY NIGHT SOLDIER

JOHN SIMINSON

JANUS PUBLISHING COMPANY
London, England

First published in Great Britain 1994
by Janus Publishing Company
Edinburgh House
19 Nassau Street
London W1N 7RE

British Library Cataloguing-in-Publication Data.
A catalogue record for this book is available
from the British Library.

ISBN 1 85756 117 1

Cover design by Harold King

Phototypeset by Intype, London
Printed and bound in England by
Antony Rowe Ltd, Chippenham, Wiltshire

Contents

1 · *The Prologue*

On leaving school I joined the Rover Scouts. I was liked but was so immature and soft that I was wide open to continual teasing and I wanted out. I couldn't take it. I decided to join the Royal Wiltshire Yeomanry (RWY).

Why the Royal Wiltshire Yeomanry – a cavalry regiment? I knew nothing about horses. It could have been the Wiltshire Regiment – infantry. I wasn't fond of walking. The troopers in the RWY were a better class of person and I knew a few of them. On the other hand, my grandfather, a farmer, was a sergeant in the regiment in the Boer War in South Africa.

Having decided to join the RWY the first move was to be sworn in and then have a medical examination. A Dr Hodges was appointed for this work. It was a very cursory business and I didn't have to strip off and so he did not see that I had a small hernia. To me at that time it was a mere nothing. At school I enjoyed cricket and loved hooking or gliding the ball on the leg side when batting. On one particular day I missed the ball, a fast one, and it hit me in the groin. It was quite painful. The headmaster took me aside and looked at where the ball had hit me. I presumed there was no injury because he never said anything. Later on this omission served to my benefit.

The next procedure was to be measured for a uniform; in particular jodhpurs. The full kit comprised a great warmer, jacket, jodhpurs, peak cap, puttees, black boots, spurs and bandolier. The bandolier was made of leather and used for carrying ammunition. I reckoned it could hold at least forty-five rounds of 0.303 ammunition. In fact, at a push you could probably get ninety rounds in it. That would have been a bit too heavy for me to remain active. Putting on the puttees was quite difficult. They had to be wound round the legs and they started just below the knee. A separate browny-coloured strip of material was wound round the bottom of the puttee to hold it in place. I remember that the first time I was to parade in uniform I had to be seen by the troop sergeant. It was an Armistice Day parade. I had two strips of browny material on each leg. The top ones were quickly disposed of.

Training was carried out on Thursdays at the Territorial hall. In charge was a full-time regular soldier, a staff sergeant, surnamed Barker. His nickname was Snowy because of his very light-coloured hair. He was married and he had the use of a house adjoining the TA hall. It was a cushy job for him.

In case you are not aware, the yeomanry at that time rode horses into battle. I hadn't given much thought or concern to that. The concern came later. We used to parade in the hall, each with a sword, and had to stand with our legs apart, as though seated on a horse. Then the order would be 'right cavalry engage'. You had to point the sword so it would pierce the throat of a mounted cavalryman coming towards you! On the other hand, it would be 'left cavalry engage' or 'right infantry engage', or 'left infantry engage'. The staff sergeant would come and check you were making a suitable angle with the sword! The whole procedure seemed to me to be the height of absurdity. However, if it came to the real situation I think I would have been frightened out of my wits.

Rifle shooting practice was my favourite exercise. There was a twenty-five-yard shooting range adjoining the hall. I took pleasure in lining the sights up to the best of my ability. The ammunition was just 0.22 inches and the rifles didn't kick. Later on the squadron paraded at an outdoor shooting range near Wilton. The whole morning was spent at 200-yard and 300-yard distances using Lee Enfield rifles and 0.303 inch ammunition. It was a good day out and used up most of Sunday. I liked snap-shooting best. You were given five rounds of ammunition. Instead of the usual target, a rounded board a bit bigger than the size of a man's head would be pushed up above the parapet. It would stay there for five seconds, be removed for a short time and then come up again. I was pleased I could get four bullets on target out of five shots. You could say that it amounted to four bullseyes or four dead men – a gruesome thought. I didn't do so well on ordinary target practice. Having plenty of time to align the sights, my muscles would tire and I would lose my grip and lose accuracy.

In the springtime on a Sunday we used to travel from Warminster to Trowbridge to the Royal Horse Artillery Barracks. There were plenty of horses for us to practise riding. However, they had hard mouths, having drawn gun carriages and artillery guns. The carriages held the ammunition. This was a regular army unit. There was plenty of room at the barracks for several riding groups. The horses were already saddled-up and bridled ready for us to ride. There were usually three groups and riding instructors were employed to put you under test, to assess your ability and teach you skills. For some idiotic reason I was put into an advanced riding group; it was said I had a good seat in the saddle. After the second week the advanced ride had to go through the jumping pen. The pen was about thirty yards long and three yards wide, with an entry at one end and an exit at the other. There were two brushwood fences about two feet high; well spaced out. As soon as they entered the pen the horses would gallop wildly across the fences. Only one horse and rider would go at a time. You had to let go of the reins and hold on to a strap round the horse's neck. I came off every time and it was a wonder that I didn't get injured. So much for my good seat in the saddle. I don't recall receiving any help or instruction on how to cope with jumping horses.

The yeomanry camp was held every year in the early summer. It lasted two weeks and was a time to gain experience as a cavalryman, also an essential part of training. Well, I funked it. I couldn't possibly face up to the camp and refused to attend the first one. It caused quite a furore. I wondered if I was a marked man but there was nothing to show that I was.

The time for the second camp came round for me and I had to go; there was no escape. It was held just outside Worthing. The weather was good which made life quite pleasant. However, looking after your equipment, saddlery, rifle etc, was hard work, besides caring for your horse. Reveille was sounded by a trumpeter. The horse usually came first. The animal had to taken from the horse lines to be fed from a nosebag and then watered. You went for breakfast next, wash and shave. Then came dressing up in your full uniform, collecting blanket, saddle, rifle, rifle bucket and harness to go to the horse lines. Saddling up was quite an art and it came first. The saddle blanket and saddle were carefully placed on the horse's back. The girth strap went round under the horse's belly and it had to be pulled up and buckled quite tight. One had to be careful that the horse hadn't blown out its stomach or else the saddle would slip round when the stomach returned to its normal size. Next came the surcingle, a long strap that went round the girth and the saddle. You then removed the halter and put on the bridle harness, bit and reins. Usually it wasn't too much bother. Then you marched with the rifle in your left hand and led the horse with your right hand to the parade ground.

Mounting your horse was quite difficult. The rifle was put between your legs as you turned to face the saddle. The reins were pulled up together in your left hand and the rifle in your other hand was swung over the saddle. The rifle was temporarily held in your left hand with the reins, while your left foot was put in the stirrup. You then gripped the saddle with your left and right hands. With one big heave you pulled yourself into the saddle, then leaned forward and swung the rifle in your right hand backwards and slid it into the rifle bucket. The bucket of course, was fixed to the right-hand side of the saddle. At this point quite a few things could go wrong. The saddle could slip round and you with it. The horse was not used to this strange treatment and could rear up, bolt forward or generally misbehave. It was important, of course, to hold on to the reins and get control of the animal. At camp the horses were mostly hired on contract and were usually a very mixed bunch of varying personalities. Some of the yeomanry were farmer's sons or farmers and had their own horses. They were the lucky ones.

After the morning parade and cavalry exercises all the horses were fed and watered. The saddlery was put away. Next came the grooming of the animal with a firm hairbrush. After-wards the horse would stand in its line with halter and blanket on. The blanket reached from the neck to the hindquarters and one hind leg would be shackled down to the ground. The shackle is a leather strap with a buckle fixed to the leg and a short rope hanging from it would be pegged into the ground.

Having left your horse recovering from the morning exer-cise, you had time for a beer. There was always a beer tent at camp. The first pint went down without hesitation – it felt good. After the mid-day meal the afternoon was spent busily cleaning all the harness, stirrups, horse's bit and all the buckles and brasses. It was hard and tiring work.

If you were not on guard on the horse lines you were free to go out. I remember going to the cinema once and falling asleep as soon as the film started. I woke up at the National Anthem and found there was no chance for a refund of the admission fee. The camp that was held at Worthing gave me a chance to enjoy ice skating at Brighton Ice Rink. Good food was an added interest. At Brighton I had a mixed grill at an excellent restaurant for four shillings and sixpence.

Another yearly event was the yeomanry dinner – usually held at Salisbury. It was always a good nosh-up and there was plenty to drink. There were speeches and reports from various mem-bers of the regiment and a song from one of the troopers.

2 · *The Real Thing*

August 1939 came and it altered all our lives. For me it was an adventure that lasted six and a half years. I was nearly twenty-two years old and twenty-eight when I was discharged – a vast chunk out of my life. My father said to me it would seem like a bad dream. My brother, Lawrence, had joined the regiment the year before and we went off with the RWY to Netheravon to guard aeroplanes at the aerodrome. War had not yet been declared, but preparations were being made for it. We were billeted in a large hall at the RAF barracks. When we were on guard duty we slept in a hut quite close to the planes. It was very uncomfortable, with just one blanket laid on the wooden floor. I found it very eerie walking round the buildings and the planes on my own in the middle of the night. Guard duty meant two hours on and four hours resting. The planes there were the Wellington bombers which were used in the first bombing raid on Germany.

There were rumours, as ever during wartime, of a spy in the district. At another aerodrome nearby a cow had been shot dead. On guard at night if you came across somebody or something moving you had to say, 'Halt, who goes there?' If there was no satisfactory answer you then had to say 'Halt, or I'll fire.' The poor cow couldn't answer and died on the spot.

On 3rd September, a Sunday, we all gathered in the refreshment canteen to hear the Prime Minister, Neville Chamberlain, at 11a.m. He announced he had had no reply from Germany and a state of war now existed between the two countries. It came as no surprise.

After a few days other troops came and took over our duties. We were on the move to Wincanton. Warminster troop had a room in the hut at the back of the old primary school. Lawrence, my younger brother, and I bought an old mattress to sleep on because it was a very rough floor. The main school was used for the squadron office and NCOs' quarters. Meals were taken at a vacant house in the main street of the town. Through lack of good organisation there were complaints at first about poor meals, but it was quite pleasant living in the town as the pubs were quite good and handy. Another advantage was that Warminster, our home, was not far away so we were able to get home alternate weekends and, thanks to an NCO from Warminster, it worked out very well. We would leave Wincanton by car on Saturday morning and return Monday morning.

The daily routine, of course, soon commenced as the horses arrived. The whole regiment occupied Wincanton Racecourse and the fields adjoining it. Our troop was stationed in a fifteen-acre field immediately adjoining the racecourse. The horse lines consisted of heavy posts dug into the ground about thirty feet apart. Specially linked lengths of rope were joined together and fastened between the posts; the horse lines. At the road end of the field there was a drinking trough which was protected by posts round both sides. In a shed adjoining the field harness and saddlery were stored. Reveille was at 5.45a.m. each morning and we used to march in a group to the field which was about one and a half miles away. Quite often we sang a popular ditty or song. The horses would have a light feed and then be taken to be watered. We would then return to have breakfast, have a wash and get dressed in uniform to return to the field in an orderly manner. Then came the saddling up, unshackling the horse's leg and untying the halter rope tied to the line. The halter was removed and the harness put on. We were then ready to set off for whatever action was ordered.

A memorable exercise was arranged for the main racecourse area. The horses were harnessed as usual but with no saddle. The saddle blanket was put on the horse's back, but it was held in place by a surcingle. In a way it seemed more comfortable than riding with a saddle. We did various exercises; wheeling and splitting up in groups, both at a trot and canter.

My horse was very big and seemed comparatively quiet. She was very ticklish and couldn't bear the dandy brush going up inside her leg. One day she seemed more settled than usual and so I worked the brush higher up the leg than ever. I paused for a moment. Then suddenly she lashed out and knocked the brush out of my hand. I never made that effort again. It could have caused me an injury.

One wet day our troop set off in single file, and we had to wear a groundsheet to keep us reasonably dry. The sheets were designed to be used as a cloak, but some of the buttons were missing. Mine was flapping about and before I knew what was happening the horse had the bit between its teeth. I couldn't control the animal. It was frightening. We went down the whole length of the field at a gallop and jumped over the water trough. There was a low hedge and then the hard road twenty-five feet further on. The horse did a very sharp turn left and I fell off landing on my back. I couldn't stand up. Somebody sent for a stretcher and I was taken to the first aid tent. I don't remember what happened there, but I was riding again the next day.

Despite some of my experiences with horses, I felt sorry for them. Here they were, pegged out in the open and tied to a line in all weathers. The only protection was a horse blanket. Furthermore, it was autumn and everything became cold and wet. The ground became a soggy mess of mud. I have stood in four to six inches of mud grooming my horse. It was soon discovered that some of the horses were not strong enough to carry a cavalryman complete with a sword, a rifle and a bag of feed, so they were returned. Worse still, some horses developed 'strangles'; an animal's form of pneumonia. Some of them had to be put down.

Towards the end of November the RWY was moved to the Nottinghamshire area. I presume the idea was to find a better situation for the horses – under cover. At Nottingham I was able to visit the theatre and see a performance of the musical comedy *The Belle of New York*. It was a treat for me. It is a show that is hardly ever performed now by amateurs or professionals. The regiment's stay here could only be for a brief time as it was going to the Middle East in January. On arrival there the horses were sold and light tanks were produced. What a shock for the troopers. Personally I was not involved, as, after a medical check, it was discovered I had a hernia. I was medical category deferred. My brother also left the regiment as he was under age for overseas service. He was transferred to the Royal Corps of Signals. It was that particular corps because of his normal employment in the GPO.

In December I was transferred from RWY to the 4th Cavalry Training Regiment at Colchester. Now I really began to feel like a regular soldier and not a Saturday night one. What a transformation it was; well-built army barracks and no mud. The barracks were spotless, with sprung bedsteads, pillows and blankets. There were regular army NCOs and men but also new recruits. In addition, like me, there were those who were unwanted for some reason or another in other regiments. The regular army corporal in my barrackroom was quite a card. He divided us up into groups – some were Goons and others were Jeeps.

Life seemed to be something of a jumble. Nothing particular was happening. However, one day I was interviewed by an officer and, because of my experience as a clerk and shorthand typist, I was made the squadron clerk. An office was set up in one of the rooms adjoining a barrackroom. This room was usually used as an NCOs' bedroom. I was allowed to sleep in my office, what luxury. It was now a week or two before Christmas and some of us were allowed a week's leave – what luck.

The train journey from Colchester to Liverpool Street station, London, was quite good. Then it was a trip on the underground to Paddington station. I was not used to the underground. The journey from Paddington to Westbury, Wiltshire, was long and trying. It was night-time. The blinds were drawn because of the blackout and the lighting was poor. There were several stops of the train and it was difficult to tell where we were because it was mostly in the country. Eventually I arrived home at Warminster and it was great to be back.

After Christmas it was back to Colchester. The barracks were practically part of the town. It was not too far to the centre. I was out most nights of the week. I had brought back my 'blues' walking out uniform and it made life easier to get dressed to go out. However, the Regimental Provost NCO frowned on it. At weekends I used to get into full cavalry kit. That included wearing the bandolier, jodhpurs and puttees. The pubs were quite good. I became friendly with a local man and had many interesting conversations with him. His views on politics and war were quite reasonable. After the pubs shut you could get a hot snack on the way back to the barracks – egg and bacon – one shilling and sixpence. Life was really pleasant. I joined the local Amateur Operatic Society. Singing is my favourite hobby and I was readily accepted into their company. On the other hand, when I called at the choir vestry of the local church after evening service nobody seemed to want me. However, I paid a visit to the local Congregational Church and I sang there.

At the start there was not a lot of work to do. I spent time brushing up on my typing skills and also my shorthand. The Squadron Leader, a Captain Black, was a very pleasant man. One of the regular officers thought that as a bit of fun he would test out my training as a TA soldier. He arranged for me to meet him at the barracks' indoor rifle range. I was given a rifle and some rounds of 0.22 ammunition. He said I could have a sixpence for each bullseye I got. Well, having shot two bullseyes, he started stamping on the board beside me. I finished up with two bulls, two inners and a magpie. He handed over a shilling. I think he was expecting me to be a poor shot, but he had received a surprise.

Life in the barracks was reasonable. You got use to bugle calls at certain times of the day. The food, not marvellous, was at least edible. There was a NAAFI but I don't remember using it. Lights out was at 10.15p.m. every night. One night I had to go on guard duty. One attended at the guard house which was at the entrance to the barracks. The duty was to walk round the stables where the horses were quartered; the usual two hours on and four hours off. There was very little to it really. After a time I stopped walking and had a short lie-down on a bale of straw. When I got back to the guardroom I had a wisp of straw sticking out of my cap. The guard commander created. I managed to get out of trouble and denied I had been failing in my duty.

Unexpectedly, one officer appeared to like me and christened me with a soppy nickname, 'Bright Eyes'. It stuck for a time but I found it very embarrassing. I couldn't object. Nobody else used this name, luckily.

There had to be a Sergeant Major in the squadron. The man who was chosen was a regular soldier recalled to the colours. His previous service had been as a Farrier Sergeant Major. A farrier's job is shoeing horses. This one's experience and knowledge of administration was very limited; however, we managed to get along fairly well.

In May 1940 I was able to get a week's leave at home in Warminster. However, the joyful change was rudely interrupted. The Germans had invaded The Netherlands. Everybody on leave was recalled to barracks. On arriving back at Colchester I was surprised to find that the squadron was moving out to a farm about two miles away. All the men, officers and horses were going. I was to be left behind in my office, but my peaceful life did not last long. The Sergeant Major looked inside the office one day and decided it was not tidy enough. I was moved out and a squadron office was arranged in a downstairs room at the farmhouse.

Life took on a different pattern now. No bugle calls; a bar for alcoholic drinks was set up in the barn. A stand was erected to take two barrels of beer. I was allowed to 'tap' one. I was keen to do it but a little apprehensive of making a 'cock-up'. With the beer tap in my left hand and a heavy mallet in my right I struck. It was a success and gave a big boost to my confidence.

Guard duty was now necessary for everyone. On my turn it felt very spooky, as it was a very lonely place. There was a searchlight platoon nearby, but they seemed to see little action. There was a directional search unit to help find the planes, an idea that appeared to be an archaic affair. I did not know about radar then.

On Saturday nights I used to get a lift or a bus into Colchester. Mostly I went on my own. It became a pub crawl most times. I could drink eight pints of bitter, walk back to the farm, about two and a half miles, and sleep very soundly until 8a.m. the next day. During the week I used to go to a pub about a mile from the farm. You had to cross several fields to get there and on the way back you could see the anti-aircraft barrage over London. At the time I don't remember feeling for the people in London suffering from the bombing. I suppose it seemed very remote and we hadn't had any experience of bombing at that time.

The stay at the farm lasted about two months, but then came an important change. At the end of the First World War it became obvious to a number of people that cavalry were really unsuitable for modern warfare. The invention of tanks, armoured cars and aircraft had changed the battle action. But still there were men being trained for the cavalry, including the Territorials. It was not until 1927 that the first cavalry regiment was changed over to using armour. The delay can be attributed to financial stringency and also a conservative attitude among the senior command. In 1939 twenty cavalry regiments became armoured overnight! The title for these regiments was Royal Armoured Corps. At that time there was a British Cavalry Division in the Middle East. No wonder my old regiment, the RWY, were sent to the Middle East with their horses. The only horsemen left now are the squadrons of the Household Cavalry. It is interesting to note that in 1950 President Harry Truman signed a bill that officially abolished horse cavalry in the United States.

I haven't any strong recollection of the move out of the farm at Colchester. I remember travelling by train across country and then to Tidworth, Wiltshire. Here we were on the famous Salisbury Plain. It was grand to be living in my home county and not that many miles from home. The barracks were fairly old and ours was the farthest from the town! It was named Aliwal. We were now titled the 61st Training Regiment RAC. The staff in some cases had to be replaced to cope with the new training. To begin with there were no recruits. The staff had to perform guard duties. There was a hill adjacent to the barracks which was of a good height. I remember being on night guard at this point. From the top you could see for many miles, even at night. I always looked up at the stars to find the Plough and the North star.

The squadron office was set up in what was originally an NCO's bedroom. It was a similar situation to that at Colchester. This time, however, there was an office next door for the Squadron Leader and Sergeant Major. The barrackrooms and the dining hall were only a few steps away, which was very convenient. I was allowed to sleep in the office where the office furniture comprised only two tables and a large cupboard. There were also two chairs, a few trays and a typewriter. When the recruits arrived for training life became very busy. There would be about a hundred men on each draft. The details of the men, for example, army number, next-of-kin and home address, would come from the Regimental Office. A record of each group or draft had to be kept. Besides the details I have mentioned there had to be a note of each man's religious denomination, date of birth and medical category. AB64s had to be made out for each man which contained all the aforementioned information plus details of training courses, etc. When the soldiers left the regiment they would take their AB64 with them. When the men went on leave all the passes and rail warrants had to be made out. When the squadron was up to full strength I was allowed a clerk to help cope with the work. Although I was well experienced as a clerk, I decided to take the official army test when it came available. The test was set by the chief clerk at the Regimental Office. On my record it said 'Passed test clerk grade III'. This information proved very convenient for me later when I arrived in the Middle East.

It was very interesting to note that each group of recruits came from the same area. The first six weeks were spent on basic training, for example, marching, arms drill, PE, and firing on the range, etc. The men would then be considered for different jobs, for instance – gunner, driver, driver-operator, and mechanic, I think the full training lasted three months, though it was brief compared with peace-time training.

Every so often the Regimental Office would issue orders. There were Part One orders which would cover general information and Part Two orders would cover such items as movement of NCOs and men, promotions, and courses for various reasons. These orders would be brought round to the squadron offices by the Orderly Sergeant – a permanent position. He was a very useful individual. Quite often he would bring round rumours of future happenings. If it was bad news it would be referred to as a red light and would be a green light for something good. He used to be willing to 'run' messages and procure items for you. The highlight for me each week was my visit to the Garrison Theatre, but it was a long way from the barracks. The Orderly Sergeant used to book a seat for me. The acts, of course, were supplied by ENSA and were quite good. There was no cinema in Tidworth, which was disappointing. However, there was a dance in the gymnasium every week. The band was quite good but too noisy for me. A basic supply of alcohol was available at the bar. At one dance I met a girl who worked at the GPO. I quite liked her but she was not keen on making a date; so that was that. I met her again much later on but it was too late. The regiment was moving in a few days. She was now apparently interested in getting together.

Soon after the drafts of recruits started arriving a new Squadron Leader was appointed to our squadron; a certain Major Field Marsham who was a particularly pleasant officer. I got along with him very well. I was made a paid Lance Corporal and later an unpaid acting Corporal. The Major was an ex-pupil of Marlborough. He was keen on cricket and wanted to raise a team to play a school team at Marlborough, which was not far from Tidworth. I volunteered to act as wicket-keeper. I don't know why, because I had never played in that position before. On the appointed Saturday we set off. We were really no match for the school second eleven, but the game was played in a good spirit Despite some good wicket-keeping gloves my fingers went through hell. They kept getting dislocated, but I managed to sort them out. A very nice tea was laid on and much appreciated.

There was another trip to Marlborough but not for cricket. The powers that be decided that in an invasion or some sort of emergency the staff had to take up a position in Marlborough High Street. One Saturday we set off for the weekend. It was an incredible sight because the squadron office was set up in a public house in the main street. It was to be the centre of communications.

Now at this time there was a shortage of cigarettes. One of the recruits was of Jewish extraction and offered to go home to London at weekends to get a supply of them as he had plenty of contacts. He was allowed to see the Squadron Leader who decided that the idea could be tried out. It was very nice for him to have every weekend away. However, he had to work for it. On Monday mornings the cigarettes were sold from my office window. They were a very wide range of brands. The scheme worked well.

I had two or three leaves home from Tidworth while I was there. Travelling was quite simple – just two buses, one to Salisbury and another on to Warminster. During one of my leaves the Americans arrived and their tanks were clogging up the streets and roads.

Father's music business was just ticking over. Fortunately he had a small income from his position as organist at the Minster Church. Mother was concerned about my sister who had TB and was in hospital at Winsley, Bradford-on-Avon. I went to visit her and she seemed quite happy under the circumstances, though she was confined to her bed. Later on Father became ill and was in hospital for treatment, so Mother was now travelling to two separate hospitals and trying to keep the shop going. She did a marvellous job.

I was now getting fed up with my hernia. I am not sure really that was the cause of my wanting to move on, but certainly some impulse was pushing me on. The Sergeant Major in particular wanted me to stay. I could have stayed there for the rest of the war. My father had a hernia in the First World War but he did not have the operation. His had been caused through moving pianos around and now he always wore a support to hold the bulge in place.

3 · *To Fitness and Duty*

I was admitted to Battle Hospital, Reading, which appeared to be an efficient place. There were voluntary visitors to the wards on certain days. One old lady who spoke to me had known my uncle at Tenterden, Kent. He was a character and owned a flourishing garage business. I heard he once lit a cigarette with a five-pound note – what extravagance.

I don't remember having any trouble before or after the operation, but I was not allowed to stand or walk about for three weeks. This operation is a different story nowadays. I was transferred to an auxiliary hospital at Bucklebury after ten days. Here was luxury indeed. It had been a beautiful country house; in fact, it still was, but had been temporarily converted. The bathroom was tiled from floor to ceiling and what a beautiful bath it had. Auxiliary nurses (VAD) were on duty. The food was excellent. In the main hall there was a full-size snooker table, so some of the patients and I had some excellent games of billiards; I even won a competition. Next I was sent to a convalescent unit at Westbury, Wilts – just three and a half miles from home – what luck! Life was a doddle here. I helped out at the administration centre. The place had been a private school for secondary pupils before the war. There was a good theatre on the site and I saw some talented amateur entertainment there. Mine was a comparatively short stay at Westbury. Soon I was back at Tidworth.

On returning to the regiment I was now classed as A1 fit and had to start training. Somebody else was already in my

job. I decided I wished to train as a driver/operator. I was
exempt from basic training, however, PE was still on the time-
table. In the gymnasium I could manage the ground exercises,
but when it came to climbing a rope hanging from the ceiling
I was done for. One of the PE instructors knew my background
and helped me out.

At this time the regiment was moved to Barnard Castle – a
long way from home. The buildings were all recently built.
The nearest town of any size was Darlington. Every Saturday
with a couple of mates I used to travel there on a bus for a
good meal and to go to the pictures. It was an enjoyable time.
The food in the barracks was very good. It was here that I
discovered my enjoyment of liver and bacon.

As a driver/operator you had to learn to drive a jeep, thirty-
hundredweight, lorry, Bren gun carrier and a tank. The Bren
gun carrier was the hardest. The steering was done with a
wheel as on a car or a truck. However, it was a continual fight
to keep the carrier going in the direction that you wanted to
go. Even on a bend or when going straight you had to battle.
On a day out practising driving, the driver on the carrier in
front of me must have lost patience. He yanked the wheel over
too sharply and he demolished part of a drystone wall. The
tank driving practice came next but it was very brief. In fact,
it lasted only half an hour. The steering on a tank is done by
two levers, one for each track. Each lever has four positions –
ordinary drive, track disengaged, slow drive and track locked.
You might say therefore, not a great deal of control. However,
I have found out since that modern tanks run on the same
system. Needless to say, on my short drive on a tank I broke
one of the tracks. I was too slow to stop when ordered. I did
not do very well on the thirty-hundredweight truck either as I
was very careless. In my civilian life I had had no experience
in driving at all – except on the dodgem cars. However, I
would only be expected to drive any vehicle in an emergency.

My main occupation was to be a wireless operator, a job
which really interested me. As a teenager I had built a radio

from instructions. Also I had designed and built a two-stage, low frequency amplifier. The amplifier was to provide record music at the silent film shows I use to give. It was also used later on to play records in my father's music shop.

I can't remember in which order the course ran. However, the most difficult part I found was tuning the set to a fixed frequency. The sets worked on the short wave band. There would be plenty of frequencies to tune to. The aerial was a metal rod – probably of copper. The set would be worked from a twelve or twenty-four volt battery. For practising the sets would be fixed in several fifteen-hundredweight trucks. Now for the crux of the matter. One person on one set would be control and would set up his set for a certain frequency. The control then sent out his signal and the rest of the sets had to be tuned into it. Now it needed great care for to me it seemed you could lose your tuning. When everybody had tuned in all the trucks would set off as though on some exercise. You had to keep in touch with control all the time. Communication was by speech. We used to drive through hilly countryside and sometimes if you were in a valley the signal used to fade out or get lost. What fun!

To me it seemed extraordinary that, having used speech on the radio, we had to learn Morse. I enjoyed this exercise even so. We had to reach a speed of at least twelve words a minute on receive. There was never any exercise or practice to send messages by Morse. In fact most of us reached at least fifteen words per minute and later on faster still. It was straightforward to me to listen to the Morse Code, but we had a brief practice watching it on a signal lamp. I just found it very difficult to tell what the flashes meant. If there had been sufficient time to get used to it all would have been well.

Fitness was not forgotten. One strenuous effort was to walk and run one hundred yards alternately for ten miles. Surprisingly, I did quite well. Life was really interesting and purposeful. Then it was all over and we were off by train again.

We arrived at Bovington Camp in Dorset. It was a long

march with full kit from the station to the camp, also very tiring after a long train journey. The buildings were rather old and tatty. There was no serious training but we were kept well occupied. Then came embarkation leave. I did not let it become an emotional time. I went out for drinks most nights. My cousin Olive was a good companion on a couple of occasions. My mother was brave and thoughtful. I visited my sister Peggy who was still in Winsley Sanatorium. She appeared quite well. It was to be the last time I saw her. I considered her my favourite relation. Then it was the day of departure. My mother came out to see me walk up to the station. My father accompanied me and saw me onto the train. We did not say very much.

At the barracks there was still some light training. Then came inoculations. I developed a severe pain in my side, above the waist. The doctor thought it would go away, but no luck. After a few days I went to see the MO again. This time he arranged for a very large piece of sticky bandage to be put around the area of pain. It was an enormous size. I have never seen one as big as that before or since. It certainly cured my discomfort. I let it stay on for about two weeks. I think the trouble must have been caused by worry or anxiety. However, I have never had that pain again. Nobody else in our group appeared to have any trouble like mine.

Despite the fact that we were waiting to go for overseas service we were not confined to barracks. My friend Ken Rider and I had a very enjoyable trip to Bournemouth. It is not very far from Bovington. We saw a good film and had a tasty meal.

4 · *Overseas Service*

About ten days before Christmas our draft moved to the railway station. It was a long journey and at the end of it we found ourselves at Liverpool docks. It was a dull and dreary day as we embarked on a New Zealand liner named the *Rangitiki*, which was of nearly 17,000 tonnage. I did not take very long to set settled in and to be introduced to the hammock and life safety belt. The hammock was really comfortable for sleeping and I enjoyed it. I found myself in charge of the meals table which had about twenty places. The food was quite reasonable. We were on the port side of the ship – aft. After a meal we settled down for a good night's sleep. It had been a very long day and it was late. The ship set sail overnight so I did not see us moving out of the docks.

The next day was a time for discovery. You were free to go on deck at any time; a freedom which I enjoyed very much as it was so very stuffy down below. The vessel was steaming up the North Sea but no land was in sight. Other ships were joining us to make up a convoy. We passed through the North Channel out into the Atlantic Ocean. Then along came our protection – several destroyers. It was fascinating to watch the craft signalling to one another. Special lamps were employed and Morse Code was used. I found it too difficult to read the messages as it was too fast for me.

After a few days of leaving Liverpool the convoy was heading due west out into the ocean. There was a fierce gale blowing. The seas were very heavy. The ship was heaving up and down and most of the men were ill. I was determined not to be sea-sick. It helped to go up on deck, despite the raging of the sea. We had sailed from Liverpool on 17th December. Now it was 25th December, and only two of us out of twenty sat down for Christmas dinner. It was a time I shall never forget. Eventually we were steaming south into quieter conditions. During the whole voyage there was never any real sign of enemy action against us. I presume the rough weather was too much for the German submarines or they had gone home to celebrate Christmas.

The weather was now getting warmer the further south we travelled. Then we arrived at Freetown, the main port of Sierra Leone, West Africa. The stop was for supplies. The town was on one side of the harbour but mostly it was surrounded by tropical vegetation. That was forty-nine years ago so I imagined it must have changed by now. But not so; just recently I saw some film of Freetown on the television and it looked just as backward. The natives came out each day in their weird boats or canoes to shout for money. The squaddies threw their pennies or what-have-you into the water. It was a drop of about thirty feet. The natives were marvellous at diving for the cash in the water and I don't know who enjoyed it most, the soldiers or the natives. We spent New Year's Eve in the port. All the ships sounded their sirens at midnight though there was no special celebration.

After a few days the convoy set sail again – going south. We were getting nearer to the Equator. It was so warm I used to sleep on deck. Fetching food from the ship's galley was a trying job. It was so hot and stifling down there that one felt great respect for the cooks and assistants. The surface of the sea had become very still. It had become like a giant mirror; hardly a ripple was to be seen. On maps of the world showing directions of various winds, this region is called the doldrums. Sailing ships used to get stranded here.

The day we were crossing the Equator there was the usual 'Crossing the line' ceremony. There was a big pool of water between the superstructures of the ship. All people crossing the line for the first time are ducked in the pool by Father Neptune. He is the Roman God of the seas. It was a great day of hilarity. I don't expect there's much call for this performance now, as surely everybody travels by air. Perhaps the pilot of the plane announces the fact that the Equator is being crossed. Maybe a celebration occurs in the air.

I used to spend a lot of time watching the sea and the weather. On different occasions I spotted a whale and some sharks. Life was not completely idle. There used to be regular boat drill where we had to parade with our lifebelts on and be sharp about it. This exercise was necessary in case of abandoning ship. Physical training on the top deck was a pleasant occupation. Adjoining our mess deck there was a shower room which was very useful immediately after exercising. However, it was only sea water and you felt rather sticky afterwards.

For some unaccountable reason I lost my emergency ration on the trip under circumstances that could have been very serious. The offence meant going on a charge and I was 'up' before the Commanding Officer. I was admonished, the lightest possible punishment. The ration was in a metal container about the size of a two-ounce tobacco tin. Inside the tin was a large block of chocolate! Some emergency!

The weather was gradually altering now. It was colder and the sea became very choppy. The ship was rounding the Cape of Good Hope though there was no clear sign of land. Next we were heading north. We had arrived in the Indian Ocean. At this time there were several rumours about our destination. The ship would be docking at Durban but what was to happen next? It was possible our draft would be going to India and then Burma. The thought of the possibility worried me. I was bound to be scared of the jungle and strange wild animals.

It was now getting warmer and very pleasant. The next day we were disembarking and I was in charge of the luggage on the dock side. We were all marching along to another ship. It seemed to be a busy place. Natives were selling fruit, in particular pineapples. One crane driver was selling fifty packets of Golf Leaf cigarettes at two shillings a time. Later on the ship's canteen were selling the same at ten pence.

One of the soldiers paused for a rest by one of the storage sheds. As he sat there a bale fell on him and he was killed. It was a tragedy to die like that. I wonder what his next-of-kin thought about it. There was a middle-aged white woman on the dock side singing songs in English to cheer us on our way. It seemed to be an extraordinary performance but it was gratifying. We arrived at our next vessel. It was marvellous – the Dutch liner – the *New Amsterdam*. The accommodation was better here and it was such a big surprise. It soon came to light that we were going to Egypt – what a relief that was for me.

Then, somewhat to my surprise, some native troops came on board. The body odour from these men was very strong. I don't know which deck or situation they were installed in but I didn't even see them again. Of course, the *New Amsterdam* is very spacious.

Unfortunately I was appointed Mess Orderly once again. I had to get moving at 6.15a.m. every morning which was a very tiring job and the washing conditions were very poor.

The ship set sail from Durban at tea time on 10th January 1943. No other vessels were involved but there were three destroyers alongside as protection. The liner was moving quite quickly – at fifteen to twenty knots. After two days the destroyers left us. On the same day a storm was brewing up and, despite its size, the ship was rolling. For the first time on board ship I felt ill. I slept on the floor for a change.

The main dining hall was divided up into tables and partitions for meals and recreation e.g. playing cards. I learnt to play Auction Bridge. There were evenings of entertainment by amateur artists and on one occasion there was a Religious Brains Trust. Ken Rider was still with me and he was a good companion. I enjoyed his Lancashire brogue. He had a very kind nature. Although I had his address I regret that I have never written to him. On the other hand, he has not communicated with me. We parted company in Egypt. Just recently I thought of trying to contact him. I rang directory enquiries and asked them to trace a K Rider in the Oldham area. There was one and I dialled the number. Lo and behold, Ken answered the phone. It was remarkable; contact has been restored after forty-nine years.

The weather was improving – getting warmer. The liner was now travelling up the Red Sea. No land was visible except when we drew nearer to Egypt. Preparations were being made for the end of the voyage. Our tropical dress was going to be packed away. I couldn't believe it. Surely it was going to be very warm, at least in Egypt. However, in the event I was wrong. My battledress was all creased after having been stored in the kit bag. I laid it on the deck having first dampened it. I put a blanket on top and slept on it. It did the trick. The next day my battle dress looked quite decent. Our money had to be changed into Egyptian piastres. Also, each man had to draw a pistol. As usual there were rumours about. The driver-operators were going to their armoured cars. After ten days' sailing we had arrived at Taufiq, a port near the southern end of the Suez Canal. Despite the fact that it was war time I felt excited and intrigued at seeing a new country: Egypt.

5 · North Africa

We left the liner on a lighter – a flat-bottomed boat. Each of us was carrying both of our kit bags. On arriving at the landing stage I found it very difficult to step on to it carrying both bags. Next we were bundled on to a railway carriage. It was not long before the train set off. As soon as we had left the port enclosure an Egyptian native sprang on board and into our carriage. He had a large basket of tangerines which he obviously wanted to sell at a good profit. We wouldn't have any idea of their worth. Before he could start a sergeant rushed into the carriage and upturned the basket and the tangerines flew all over the place. The native was bundled off the train. I felt a tinge of sorrow for him.

It was an interesting train journey from Taufiq to Cairo, then to El Giza where we boarded some lorries. We arrived at our camp at 3a.m. on Sunday 30th January. The journey had taken a total of forty-five days. We were in tents on sand and went straight to sleep. I woke up at 7.35 and went outside for a look round. What a surprise to find the camp was only about one and a half miles away from the Pyramids. It was an incredible situation. Being a Sunday I was glad to have a day of rest.

The following day we were put into troops. All our webbing equipment had to be scrubbed. Then came the very important vaccination and inoculation. You never knew what germs you were going to meet. I got my hair cut. When we were free we walked down to the YMCA. Here I wrote airgraphs home. The

airgraph was a very useful means of communication. It was a
special piece of paper, nearly foolscap size. You wrote your
name, unit and MEF at the top, and whatever you wanted to
say, also your present address. The papers would be taken,
censored and photographed. I imagine it must have been on
microfilm. The film would have gone by air to England. There
it would be reproduced and sent to the recipients. It was a
good system.

A day later some of us were going to PAI Force. The following day it was cancelled! Of course, all of us were reinforcements and although we belonged to the RAC we were not in
any particular regiment as yet.

In an adjoining camp I found Ken Rider and some of the
other fellows who were at Bovington. It was a joyful reunion.
In the canteen you could hear the BBC Overseas Service and
Big Ben on the radio.

All of the troops were in tents on the sand but this was really
only a temporary measure. It was not far to a hard road. But,
astoundingly, the other side of the road was lush greenery,
palm trees etc. Beside the road there was a native buffet where
you could get a drink and a light meal. Further along the road
towards the pyramids stood the well-known Mena House Hotel,
but I shouldn't think there were any tourists staying there
then.

One day when we had some free time Fred, a new acquaint-
ance, and I set off across the sand to see the Pyramids and the
Sphinx. As we drew nearer we began to realise the scale of
the operation. The stone blocks must have been at least six
feet long and two feet six inches high and wide. The weight
of one block must have been at least half a ton. With no
modern equipment to build the stones up it must have been
a very difficult and risky operation. We were looking at one of
the wonders of the world. The tallest pyramid was built as a
burial place for King Khufu. The second was in memory of his
son, King Khafre. We also walked round to the Sphinx. The
head is shaped to represent King Khafre; the body is that of a

lion. Unfortunately the face has been spoilt through weathering. It is an excellent piece of work but not as interesting as the Pyramids. On another day Fred and I had a guided tour of the passageways and burial chambers of the tallest pyramid. There was no electricity or gas lighting in the place. The only illumination was a light held by the guide. The main structure of the pyramids was built of granite. It was hewn from the Giza plateau. Limestone from Tura was brought across the Nile and used to complete the edifice. There is a third pyramid which was erected to Men-Kan-Ra. It was started in stone, but he must have died prematurely as it was small and hurriedly completed in bricks.

The next day I was lucky enough to get a lift right into Cairo. There was a club there for servicemen called 'Music for All'. You could have a bath and a meal at a reasonable price, which was very convenient. I imagine most British Servicemen in the Middle East must have visited it at one time or another. There was one thing one had to stay alert for in Cairo which was the boot-black boys. They were out for trade – to shine up your army boots for cash. However, if you didn't want their attention they could follow and pester you. Luckily I only saw them once, and then it was in the distance. There were some good streets and fine buildings in the city. On one visit, however, I found the native quarters. It was out of bounds to British troops. As I approached the forbidden place I saw it was the most dreadful-looking sight and the smell was awful.

On the first visit to Cairo I saw a film: *They all kissed the Bride*'. The cinema was packed out, probably because it was a Saturday. I had a seat downstairs and sat right at the front. It was most uncomfortable having to lean back and tilt my head to get a reasonable view. I saw quite a number of films – mostly American – while I was in Egypt.

I have only mentioned one club for troops, but there were others. They had typical names – Victory, Tipperary, and the YMCA. I visited them all.

Some days later, after the first Cairo visit, I was sent with

thers on convoy duty to el Kebir. On arrival we were issued
with a fifteen-hundredweight Dodge truck which was loaded
up in the afternoon ready for a trip next day. The convoy
moved to Ismailia about fifty miles away. It was a nice run and
I enjoyed it. There was an outdoor cinema so I paid a visit. It
was entrancing sitting in the open air with the stars twinkling
above. The NAAFI owned the place and so everything was well
run.

The next day we were issued with thirty-hundredweight Ford
trucks. They were loaded up. I was on guard during the evening. Reveille was at 05.30 hours and after a meal we were off
to Port Said. The road was next to the railway line and alongside that ran the Suez Canal. It was a very strange sight to see
an ocean-going ship appearing to move along the ground. The
countryside was completely flat which added to the effect.
The roadway was very straight and so driving was rather boring.
However, the journey hadn't taken long before the engine was
spluttering and the truck came to a halt. The NCO in charge
soon arrived. He did not take long to decide what was the
trouble. The top of the petrol pump was removed and the
pump was full of sand. In ordinary servicing of vehicle one
wouldn't inspect the petrol pump. However, in the conditions
around Egypt it would be an obvious thing to do: dry sand can
get blown almost anywhere. The convoy had left Ismailia at
about 7.30 and arrived at Port Said at 12.30. It was my first view
of the Mediterranean Sea. The harbour was busy. However, it
wasn't long before we were on the return trip. We all piled on
to the tender. It was a rotten journey back as the engine on the
vehicle was causing trouble.

The next day we were returned to our tented existence.
Many of the men at the camp were on a big draft to India.
Two of my mates, Fred and Tommy, were on it. Fred and I
went down to the 'Desert Beauty' for a farewell meal.

The following day I was on my way as well to Abassia Barracks
in Cairo with Fred. There were quite a few of us going. We set
off on a lorry and as we approached the city we were put on

the trams. It was interesting travelling through the streets. Abassia Barracks are set in the middle of a compound. It was better really to have a decent bed and get away from the sand. Inside the compound there were various places of interest, for example – CE Church, cinema, YMCA and an open-air snack bar called Scots Corner. There were also a range of shops owned and run by Egyptians. I bought a watch for 450 piastres, worth about four pounds. It was dust and shock-proof. It was a good purchase because it lasted for many years.

On 15th February I received a cable from home with Christmas greetings. It was dated 19 December 1942. I wrote a letter-card home to mother. The same day we were vetted for a wireless course. It commenced the following day. There was a new R/T and W/T procedure to learn. It was interesting. A few days later we had a wireless test. I got seventy-six per cent of the marks. I had hoped to do better than that.

On the second evening in barracks some of us went to the camp cinema. We sat in the balcony. It was a roughly constructed building. In fact, you might say it was thrown together. The film was *I take this Woman* with Spencer Tracy and Hedy Lamarr. The film was badly worn and the sound atrocious. The projectionist must have been hopeless or else the equipment was needing overhaul. The squaddies downstairs were noisy during intervals. They were throwing orange peel and condoms about blown up like balloons.

I spent about eighteen days in the barracks at Cairo. During my stay Ken and I spent many times watching films and visiting various clubs; either in the barracks or Cairo. There was some light training going on and I got up to over eighteen words a minute receiving Morse. I heard from Sam (his nickname), my brother, and replied to him. I wrote airgraphs to my cousin Olive and a friend. Olive's husband, a regular soldier and a Quartermaster Sergeant, was in Abassia while I was there. I found out this information as I was about to leave; too late to meet him. Later I heard he had been promoted to Lieutenant Quartermaster, and was also on the move.

On 3rd March I was warned at dinner time that I would be moving at any minute. I had to draw a rifle, fifty rounds of ammunition and an extra blanket. At 9.15 in the evening the move was on; by tram to the railway station and travelling all night to Alexandria. We arrived at the Transit Camp at 7a.m. and were put into tents. There was nothing to do all day. That evening at the NAAFI there was a portable 35mm film outfit. The film show was *Dangerous Moonlight.* I was in bed by 8.30.

We were awakened next morning at 4.40a.m. Told we were moving at 6a.m. I breakfasted and put my kit together, but had no time for a wash. The lorries arrived and soon we were on the dock side at Alexandria. We embarked onto the *SS Karoa,* an Indian vessel. The accommodation was cramped. The ship was 7,000 gross tonnage, rather small.

The following morning we sailed at about breakfast time. It was 6th March. In the harbour the sea was still and smooth. As soon as the ship left the protection of the sea walls it was turning, twisting and tossing. The sea was very turbulent and rough. Nearly everyone was quickly down with seasickness. It was a revelation. I too felt a bit squeamish but was able to eat my meal.

There was a convoy as you might expect, four ships in all. Five destroyers accompanied us. Rather heavy cover, but this was the Mediterranean Sea and Italian or German submarines could have been in the vicinity. Lights had to be out each night by 7p.m.

The convoy was proceeding along the North African coastline. The destination hadn't been mentioned. Occasionally land could be seen on the port side. On the second day action stations were sounded just before dark but nothing happened. During the night the sea became very rough and was still so in the morning. On that afternoon I fell asleep on the deck and missed my dinner.

On 9th March we arrived at Tripoli. By the middle of the day the ship was anchored just outside the harbour as there were so many ships sunk in the harbour we couldn't move in.

A lighter arrived from the shore during the afternoon. The vessel was manned by black troops. I had to assist in stacking our kit on the lighter. It was not until 6p.m. that we moved off. Everything was unloaded onto a temporary landing stage. A Bofors anti-aircraft gun was in position nearby. After getting our kit together we moved to a transit camp. Supper followed and we slept in the open.

The next morning we were moved from the transit camp to No 1 Advanced Reinforcement Unit RAC. The unit was about eight miles south of Tripoli on the edge of the desert. The situation was a mixture of sand and cultivated greenery. We were all interviewed by the officer in charge. The food was reasonable; however, there was no bread, only hard biscuits. Getting nearer the sharp end, what could one expect. No clubs, shops or cinemas were available here.

At one meal every day we had to take a yellow tablet – Mepecrine. It was a malaria preventative. In that area there weren't many mosquitoes. I'm not sure whether we had these tablets while in Egypt, but for the rest of our time in Africa they had to be taken. I was lucky to escape this ghastly illness even though I had a number of bites. If you scratched the irritation it could easily become septic. Then it entailed a visit to the first aid tent or to the doctor.

The day after our arrival some of us went on a gunnery course. The officer thought we were going to be using American guns, but I managed to persuade him we should be on British ones, for example, the Besa machine gun, two-pounder and six-pounder guns. I hadn't fired the two-pounder before and I was very pleased with the result. The gun was mounted in a tank. Later on we had a wireless course. However, it seemed to me the authorities did not know what to do with us.

The accommodation for other ranks was a bivouac – a two-man tent. It was a tight fit. The weather was fine and dry so we could stay outside for longer. At night-time when there was an air raid over Tripoli there was a fine view of the ack-ack barrage.

One day there was a call for volunteers to give blood. It was a change from footling work. A three-ton truck took us into Tripoli. In a short time we had given up some of our vintage quality blood. In return we had a bottle of Italian beer which was of poor alcoholic content. I must say I felt a little dizzy afterwards – not because of the beer. The lorry took us round Tripoli for a little tour afterwards. We arrived back at camp without my tent mate – Arthur. He turned up later.

We had been at our present site about two weeks when the order came to move. It was at that time the forward troops – the famous Eighth Army – had broken through the Mareth Line and a few days later penetrated the Gabes gap. Our reinforcement until then moved forward in convoy out of Libya and into Tunisia. We settled on a pleasant spot just west of Ben Gardane. It was late at night and the bivouac tents had to be put up in the dark. The next day at about 5p.m. tea time, a sand storm blew up which lasted about half an hour. It was a question of sheltering wherever one could. Visibility was down to about fifteen yards. It was a startling experience which I did not have again. Luckily later on the meal was not affected.

About a week later the unit moved off again and arrived at Medenine. It was very pleasant here, with orchards round about and low hills. I was warned I would be moving off very shortly on draft. The next day was a Sunday. The troops were expected to attend Morning Service. Afterwards I was told I was moving – then the order was cancelled. The following day at reveille roll call I was told to be at the cookhouse at 8.15a.m. ready to move. The suspense was killing me, you might say. Of course, the Germans and Italians were in retreat. I thought there could not be a lot of fighting left!

ABOVE. Royal Wiltshire Yeomanry on Parade, 1937.

BELOW. Camp at Worthing, 1938, watering horses.

No.11.

RWY CAMP

WORTHING 1938

ABOVE. Camp Worthing, 1938, on parade.

BELOW. Warminster Troop, 1939, standing to horses, in a field adjoining
Wincanton race course.

"Pass the sand. old man!"

Cartoons of 'Two Types' concerning the 8th Army and referring to the Desert Campaign and Italy.

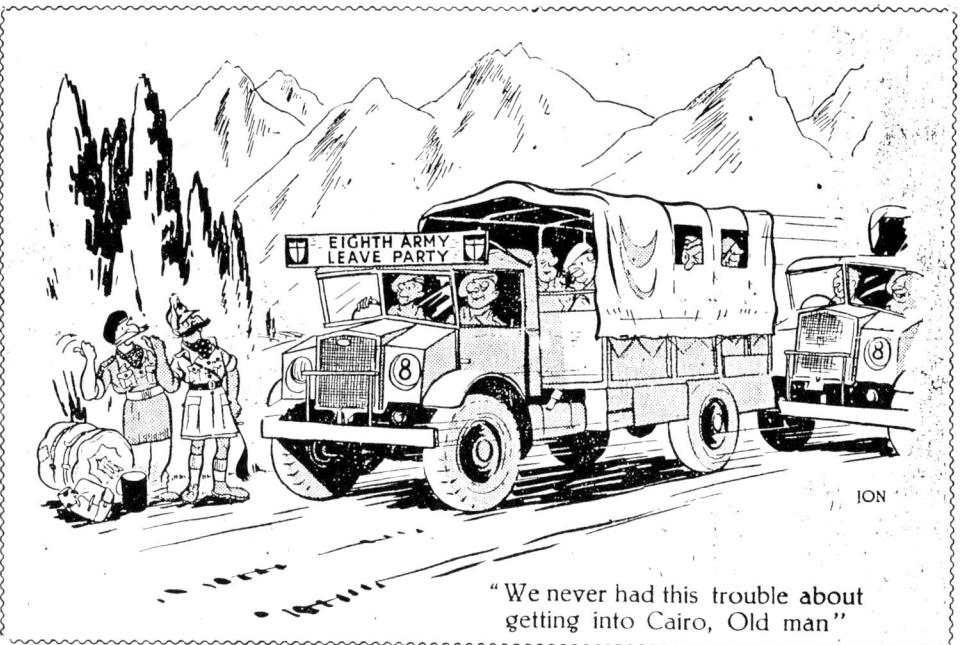

"We never had this trouble about getting into Cairo, Old man"

Last parade of 'A' squadron 4th Cavalr

aining Regiment, Colchester 1940.

The author in full uniform, Colchester, 1940.

RIGHT. Cartoon of the author as squadron clerk, 1940.

BELOW. The author and Ken Rider awaiting embarkation, Bovington 1942.

NEXT PAGE. Christmas dinner menu, Algeria 1943.

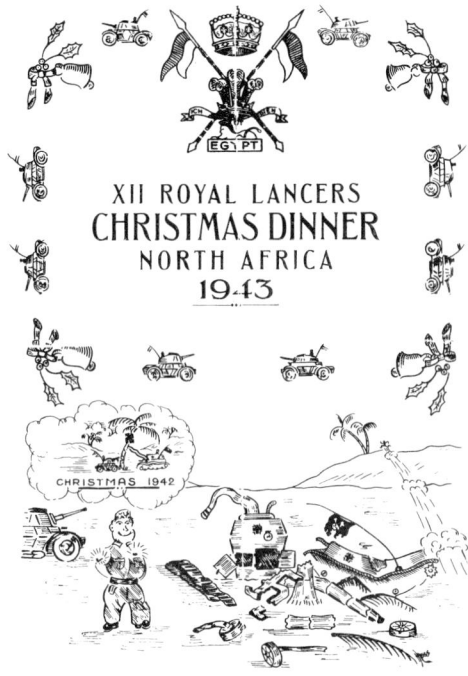

XII ROYAL LANCERS
CHRISTMAS DINNER
NORTH AFRICA
1943

MAY 1943

Roast Turkey with

Savoury Stuffing.

Roast Pork. Apple Sauce,

Roast Potatoes,

Peas — Cauliflower.

LATE WIRE :—
DON'T TIP THE WAITERS
THEY'RE ONLY SERGEANTS.

"BUT TOUCH YOUR HAT TO
THE COOKS".

Christmas Pudding

Brandy Sauce.

Mince Pies.

Nuts, Fruit — Beer — Cigarettes.

" As you were — the 've got a couple of Eighty-Eights ! "

6 · *My New Regiment*

After collecting my rations from the cookhouse and my documents at the Company Office I moved off in a lorry at 9.45a.m. We passed through the Mareth Line, or what was left of it. There were a number of German graves. I saw plenty of barbed wire entanglements and minefields marked up. There were also some unburied dead bodies lying about and the stench was awful. We arrived eventually at the 1st Armoured Division Personnel Camp. The next morning I was woken up at 4.30a.m. The artillery were laying down a barrage of shells for the next push. I spent the morning reading as I had often done when there was no activity. Eventually I was taken by lorry to the 12th Royal Lancers, 'A' Squadron. It was an armoured car unit. How was it I had always been in 'A' Squadron before and now again. The Squadron Leader gave me a short interview. He noticed from my documents that I was a qualified Army clerk as well as a driver/operator. The squadron storeman clerk wanted a change but the matter had to wait for the time being. I had to travel with 'B' echelon.

The first chance I had I sent a cable to Mother with my new address. All the time I was in the army I wrote to Mum every week whenever possible.

'B' echelon had an important task to do. There was the stores lorry on which spare equipment was kept. Records regarding troopers' pay was stored. Letters home which men had written were brought there and then despatched. It was a central point for similar activities. Some lorries were used for carrying petrol. They had about four hundred gallons on board in jerrycans: a lethal load if it gets shot up by a fighter or bomber aircraft. The driver had to pick up the petrol at a set point and take it to the armoured cars and other vehicles. A very important vehicle was the water cart. The driver had to find a suitable water supply. Mostly it was good but on one occasion in Tunisia it turned the milk a peculiar colour. There were also the food and cooks' vehicles. Most of the food was in tins, including milk. One dodge used in the desert to boil up some water was to fill a large rectangular tin with sand. Next, you poured in some petrol. The tin would have to have two sides open. You put a match to light the petrol and you had to stir the sand every so often to release some more petrol. A dodgy trick, but effective. There was also a medical aid vehicle.

I was very pleased to get more settled and with a good regiment. The troopers in the echelon were friendly and seemed decent fellows. One of the older men was full of odd sayings. He used to get at me 'Get your knees brown'. I was wearing shorts and within days the white flesh was the right colour. For the time being I had to ride on one of the petrol lorries. It was a risky business with all that petrol on board. The regiment was moving on in leaps and bounds. We had passed through the Gabes gap. Along came a lot of 'Iti' prisoners. I think they were Fascist youth. The ground we were travelling over was very rough and it was tough going. The echelon nearly landed up in the German lines. Suddenly a German ME109 fighter plane was shot out of the sky thanks to the New Zealander AA boys.

Next morning we set off again going north. Soon a German Mk4 tank came into view. Luckily for us it had been knocked out. Next we crossed a railway line. The echelon halted early in the evening. Enemy bombers came across during the evening and dropped five bombs near us.

Then we arrived at a seaside town called Sfax, a small place. With all the activity going on I thought the echelon would stay here for a time. Some trucks were unloaded. A stores office was set up in a room at an empty house. I took advantage of the sea and went for a swim as soon as I could. The waves were pounding in and it was a very invigorating experience. Unfortunately the visit was only for a few days.

The high command now decided on a change of strategy. Instead of the 8th Army as a whole proceeding north towards Tunis, a part was to be diverted and join up with the American First Army. We would be approaching Tunis from the west. One evening we came across a very deep-sided wadi – a dried up river bed. The men on the truck with me decided that an empty gun emplacement at the side of the wadi would be a good place to sleep. It was like an enormous well about seven feet deep with a diameter of twelve feet. It was decided to put the lorry tarpaulin over the top. Over a ridge about a mile away there was a hospital under canvas. As it was getting dark an enemy plane came over and dropped an aerial flare. I think it was looking for a target, but when it saw the Red Cross it went away.

One day as the echelon was up in the green hills to the west of Tunis we came across a group of Arabs. Some of the lads had acquired a little of their language. The natives wanted some tea in return for eggs, but the lads were rotten because they handed over some used tea which they had dried.

A day or two later we arrived at a sandy but rough field quite close to Tunis. There I came across some cactus growing wild for the first time. There was also some other semi-tropical vegetation in the area. I was startled and concerned when I came across an asp – a short snake.

On 12th May hostilities ceased in Tunisia.

On 16th May I visited Tunis for the first time. This involved a trip on an army truck. It seemed a quiet and pleasant city and untouched, as there hadn't been a battle for the occupation. There were some very smartly dressed women about. The wine bars were opened and I enjoyed a few drinks. A French Army band was giving a concert of music in the main thoroughfare. On my second visit a few days later I stayed all day until 4.30p.m. I did some shopping for – of all things – a bottle of ink and two rubbers. It seemed strange but the weather turned very cold and wet suddenly, yet in half an hour it had changed again and hot sunshine returned.

The very next day the Regiment moved from just south of Tunis to a point across the bay. The site was on Cape Bon. We stayed there only for about two days. The regiment moved off at 7.15a.m. on the coast road south. Our route lay through Enfidaville and then to Kairouan. We stopped south of the town for one night. Next morning we were travelling over a rough track to a hard road just south of Bou Thadi. The whole procession was now on the coast road heading for Mahres. The night was spent just north of Gabes. In the morning we followed the road through Gabes to Mareth, Medenine and Ben Gardane. It was to be Libya revisited. Our squadron was given a small farm site ten miles south of Tripoli.

The farm was occupied by an Italian farmer. There was a variety of vegetation but growing from a sandy surface. Everyone was living in small tents adjoining their vehicles. The stores and office were set up in a large tent ten feet by six feet and the cookhouse was quite handy; also in a tent.

We now had mid-summer heat and there was not a lot of shade available. The afternoon was a time of rest, a siesta for everyone.

The farmer grew his crop by irrigation and for this there was an artesian well quite handy. The water from there was pumped up into a stone-built reservoir, about fifteen feet by fifteen feet and approximately seven feet deep. There were channels going from the reservoir alongside the crops. The farmer let us have a swim when the tank was full. One day after a swim I left my swimming trunks on the sand to dry. Later when I wanted another dip I pulled my costume on and I received a sudden nip on my stomach. I immediately made an inspection. It was a baby scorpion. What a shock! I was under the impression that a bite from an arachnid could be serious; perhaps only from a fully grown one. It transpired that there were to be no ill effects.

One day we had a treat. Another of those mobile cinemas came along to give us a show. It was very much appreciated, as it was under a dusky sky and not in a stuffy cinema.

Some of the troopers who had been in the whole of the desert campaign had a grudge. Nothing was happening in the North African region so they thought they ought to have their leave in England. It was not a very ardent grumble and if it had been granted it would certainly have delayed the end of the war. Nobody would have wanted that.

I was getting down to some clerical work. The troopers were wanting money to spend so it was my job to sort out how much each man should have. The AB64 Part Two gave information on what each man was entitled to have per day. However, there was no record from the Paymaster General of what the balances were at a certain date. In some cases men hadn't received any money for weeks, but you can hardly spend money when you are on the move all the time and away from shops and towns. It was something of a nightmare and it took some weeks to sort out the mess. In some instances I had to take a chance. Eventually I drew up a book showing each man's name, army number and all possible details of pay and money entitlements.

One day my brother Lawrence came to see me. He was stationed on the coast on the other side of Tripoli. He had heard from Mother that I was in the 12th Lancers. It was a wonderful meeting. We never stopped talking – there was so much to say. At about tea time he left to thumb a lift into Tripoli. In the Royal Signals he could be attached to different regiments, or brigades or even divisional headquarters. He left North Africa before I did, spent some time in Italy but then he was sent home. On D-Day he was on the first landing on the beaches. The brigade he was with was very fortunate and Lawrence is alive and well today.

My life was not devoid of entertainment. I made two separate trips to the cinema in Tripoli. Lawrence and I had arranged to meet at a future date in Tripoli; unfortunately that failed. I can't remember why. I was offered five days' leave to 10 Corps Rest Camp but that was postponed. King George VI was inspecting 1st Armoured Division on that day. The leave came later. I remember swimming in the sea near Tripoli as being the greatest pleasure.

On Thursday 6th August the regiment moved out of Suami at 7a.m. conveyed by RASC lorries. We reached Ben Gardane by 5p.m. and encamped for the night. Next morning we were on the move again by 7.45a.m. Soon the convoy had crossed from Libya into Tunisia. The road had been improved a little between Ben Gardane and Medenine. We arrived at a spot just south of Gabes at about 2.30p.m. and parked up for the night. I went for a bathe in the sea about half a mile away. The water was lovely and warm – marvellous. The following day we moved again to a point three miles north of Sfax to take over the guard at the docks. The stores and office were billeted in part of a block of flats. The building had a flat roof from which there was a fine view in all directions.

It was a very pleasant stay at Sfax and lasted a number of weeks. However, somebody decided we had to move. It turned out to be quite a remarkable effort. The whole regiment was moved north by train! I wonder if it was to save petrol. However, when the train arrived at Tunis, everything on board had to be removed. We were bound for Algeria, but unfortunately the railway track from Tunis to Algiers was a different width. So another loading up process took place. The Tunisian track was a metre wide – three feet three inches and the Algerian track four feet eight and a half inches. I found myself in a closed in goods truck with the door left partly open. It gave me an excellent view of the countryside. The train was travelling west. It was interesting seeing the various crops and the greenery. Eventually the foothills of the Atlas Mountains came into view. It was a wonderful experience.

On arrival near Algiers lorries took us to our new billet

which was about twenty miles south of the city. It was a fairly big mill with a number of outbuildings. French troops were in occupation when we arrived. There was a tent in the yard where I was directed to go. A French soldier was about to leave. He was really friendly. It was a chance to use my little knowledge of French. I was offered a drop of wine in my mug which was just palatable. After the Frenchman had gone I noticed there was a layer of scum inside my mug. Ugh!

The situation was really pleasant away from any town and overshadowed by a very high hill. A lot of organisation had to take place. The stores and office were sited in a lean-to shed of ample size. It had to be cleared of rubbish and machinery. The floor was pretty rough, dirty and cobbled. Luckily I had a bed propped up on wooden boxes. All the stores and office equipment were set up. There were no locks on the doors. It was poor security. When winter was coming on the SQMS helped to get some heat in the place. A 45-gallon drum was cut into shape to make a stove. Some logs of wood arrived and I had a fine time with an axe cutting them up.

There was a large building which made a good place for the squadron's meals. At the other end of my lean-to there was a store. It was changed into a small bar selling a local brandy. There was a local soft drink to mix with it. It was enjoyable and I must confess I indulged myself.

The regiment up to now had always been equipped with Daimler armoured and scout cars. They were easy to drive because of their semi-automatic gear boxes. Now for some unaccountable reason enormous American armoured cars were being supplied. The general opinion was that they were unsuitable for narrow roads. In the desert where there was plenty of room they would have been fine. The gear boxes were fully automatic.

All files, pistols and sub machine guns were handed in to my storeroom. It was a responsibility, though it did not worry me. The store door was made more secure. A month or so later 'B' Squadron who were on a farm about two miles down the road had a shock. All their firearms were stolen overnight. It was said Arabs could steal the blanket you were sleeping on without disturbing you. They were expert in such clever tricks. Then, of course, there was a flap on. Immediate action had to be taken in the whole regiment. A large wooden frame arrived at my store. There were metal rods that stretched from one end to the other. The rods were spaced so that they could pass through the trigger guard on each weapon. There were padlocks on the end of each rod. I suppose you could say the weapons were reasonably safe now. Presumably everyone heaved a sigh of relief.

There was no entertainment available at the mill. However, Blida, a small town, and Algiers were not very far. There were a good number of trips arranged for these places. At Blida there was a cinema. Also there were two brothels which was quite common in French colonial countries. One was out-of-bounds to all troops and it was occupied by Arab women. The other was in bounds to British troops. It was rumoured that all the women were French officers' wives!

Algiers was an interesting place to visit. There were some good cinemas and a fine theatre. The theatre was having a show with an all-star cast of British artistes. I think there must have been a rush for tickets. It was a special performance and the place was packed out with troops. I must say, however, that I was disappointed. Two of the stars were Leslie Henson and Tessie O'Shea. It was a let-down but nothing unusual really considering the circumstances. More pleasure was gained from the various films that were available. However, one night I remember going with some others to a variety show being put on at an American unit which I greatly enjoyed because they had a lively dance band.

One evening when I had done very well on brandy I felt rather 'off', I removed my bottom set of false teeth and put them on a box at the side of my bed. When I woke up in the morning the teeth were missing. I looked everywhere but there was no sign of them. It was very embarrassing, but it obviously gave some people a good laugh. Luckily there was a dental unit in the area and transport was laid on for me to go to the dentist. He was really sensible about fixing me up with another set because a soldier is no good with nearly half his teeth missing. The story, of course, went round that a rat in Algeria was going around with false teeth.

There was a new officer who joined the squadron from Rhodesia. He was in charge of physical fitness among all the ranks. His theme centred on high tension in your muscles. With this approach I think it engendered more enthusiasm for the task. It was certainly a source of amusement.

Christmas 1943 was spent at the same location. The officers and NCOs decided that it must be good and cheerful for everybody's sake. I still have a copy of the menu which was very well produced and at some expense. A pig was produced from somewhere and I can still hear the sound of that animal in its death throes. The RSPCA would have been upset, but they weren't at hand. One of the brave sergeants had to cut its throat. I think the animal needed a different kind of ending. Anyway, Christmas was a great success.

In the middle of March 1944 the regiment was on the move again. The stay at the mill had lasted about five months. The new billet was only a temporary stop. The stores, however, were set up in a lean-to garage. It was a farm site run by a French farmer. He took me round to see some of his crops and he complimented me on my French. It was here I saw a strange sight. In an open-ended shed there sat a wooden truck, with a tree trunk fixed so that it extended outwards from it. The Arabs stood on the ground and another on the tree trunk. They held a double-bladed cross-cut saw. In this way planks of wood were being cut from the tree. I felt as if I were living in the Middle Ages.

7 · *Italy*

Within ten days we were packing everything up for the move to Italy. We arrived by truck at Algiers docks on Monday 27th April. There was a walk of a quarter of a mile carrying all of our kit which I found very hard to do. I should have joined in the keep-fit exercises. The ship waiting for us was the *Neuralia*. At a guess I think it was a 15,000-ton vessel. The washing and sanitary conditions were good, but the food was poor. We sailed on Wednesday 29th April at 10. The ship kept close to the African coast. We were in a convoy of forty ships. The following day we were joined by another twenty – sixty ships in all. On the third day in the evening two fighter planes came across to see if all was well. That night I woke up very suddenly and was astounded to find that all the hammocks were empty. My immediate thought was to wonder what was up. It couldn't have been a case of the *Mary Celeste* happening again? I swung myself out of my hammock and hurried up on deck. I was feeling very anxious. Everybody was up on deck. There had been an air raid warning, however, no aircraft had appeared or dropped any bombs.

In the morning the sea was getting very choppy. The ship was heaving and rolling a great deal. Soon we reached Sicily and entered the small port of Augusta. It was a very quiet place. The convoy sheltered there for the night, for what reason I couldn't tell. The following day, 3rd April, it was forever onward. In the distance towards the northwest I could see the glow of Mount Etna – the volcano – the largest in

Europe. The next point of interest was the straits of Messina, a narrow gap between Sicily and Italy. Soon there was another volcano to be seen but very distant – Stromboli.

On 4th April we arrived at Naples and there we were greeted with the sight of Vesuvius. I had seen three different volcanoes in as many days. The port installations were a complete shambles. American support troops were clearing the rubbish. Of course, all the damage and rubbish had been created by Allied bombers. Here the Allied troops were sorting it out – such is war. Soon all our personnel and baggage were transported to a transit camp just outside the city. It was good to have arrived safely in Italy but there was a lot of work to do. The following day we moved to a camp area for the regiment and the next exercise was the putting-up of tents. In the evening for a chance I had a game of nine-card brag. I lost twelve shillings, but I managed to get a bottle of beer. The next day a lot of tidying and cleaning up was done. Afterwards I found time to write to Mother. In the afternoon I had a visit to an American mobile bath unit which was very good. Afragola, a suburb of Naples, was quite close and my visit in the evening proved a shattering experience. The people seemed to be dressed in rags or very badly worn clothes. Food was very short. In the poorer quarters the roads were untidy and some inhabitants seemed to be tipping water out of their top window. I went to a bar for a drink where met an Italian with whom I had a brief talk in a mixture of French and Italian. I was not keen to fraternise but there was no order against it. It was a different matter in North Africa. We weren't fighting the Libyans, Tunisians or the Algerians. Here we were in the midst of the Italian people, but they had been our enemy until recently. I wonder what they really thought at the time, although I didn't come across any animosity.

There was not a great deal of work to do for a few days as none of our vehicles had arrived from North Africa. An arms check had to be made – an important item. After a couple of days everybody had to parade on a Commanding Officer's foot drill exercise with rifle. Just imagine that nothing had been done like that for a long, long time. I made a note in my diary that it was a complete shambles. It was very embarrassing for all concerned. Anyway, it filled in the waiting time.

On Saturday 15th April our vehicles arrived and were collected from the docks. Early that morning there was an air raid on Naples. I wondered if there was any connection between the two events. Now we really had started to sort ourselves out for our part in the Italian campaign. On Friday 21st April we set off in convoy going north from Naples. The road was difficult and hard; the scenery, on the other hand, was wonderful. The route led us up into the mountains and we crossed the river Volturno several times. Eventually we reached the village of Capracotta. Here we were high up in the Apennines. Thank goodness it was springtime and there was no snow about to worry us. It was a typical rugged place.

The regiment's role had now changed. Instead of scouting around searching or chasing the enemy it was just one of holding the line and was an infantry job really. There was not so much excitement and I think some of the officers and NCOs missed the adrenalin.

The village was situated on a wide ridge. The ground seemed to fall away quite quickly, especially on the side facing the Germans. There was one main street and one or two of the echelon lorries had their load of petrol cans and ammunition piled up there. The vehicles were wanted for fetching supplies.

One day I was walking along the street and I stopped to look at the pile of petrol and ammunition. To me it seemed as though there was a little petrol leaking from one of the cans. I suppose I should have reported it to someone. However, I continued my walk and called at one of the shops. Suddenly a fire started among the petrol cans and then the ammunition was exploding. What a frightening noise it made. It was devastating. I never heard who had the blame, but there were no casualties. I often wondered what the Germans across the other

side of the valley thought about it – an early firework party!
An event which happened later in that some place might lead
one to think it had been sabotage which caused the explosion.
The regiment had phone lines laid to facilitate communication
between different squadrons and regimental HQ. One day our
line wasn't operating. The Signals linesman went along the line
to see where there was a break. He hadn't gone far out of the
village when he found the line went under a rock. He pulled
on the line and this set off an anti-personnel mine. By all
possibilities he should have been killed. Some people are lucky.
The only damage done was to his foot. It was not severe and,
as they say – he'll live.

There was a shortage of most commodities in the Italian
community. I came across a young man who offered to make
me a folding bed. In return he wanted cigarettes. I think I
gave him a hundred. The bed was quite well made – light and
easy to erect. The bed lasted me right to the time we arrived
in Austria. I was really comfortable at nights now. I handed it
over to the next clerk/storeman as a gift.

In the mountains we were waiting for the big offensive and
it commenced on Thursday 11th May. In a way it was a relief.
The war had been going on for a long time. The biggest
stumbling block here was the Monte Cassino monastery situated in a high and dominating position. It was severely attacked
by gunfire and bombs but the position was held. I believe a
good few allied lives were lost in several attacks.

The Cassino monastery was eventually bypassed on both
sides. Field Marshal Kesselring ordered the retreat from this
position. Possibly he required the troops for more pressing
needs. On the other hand, they could have been cut off from
the main army.

The push was on by both the Fifth Army (American) and
the Eighth Army. The latter had a wide variety of nationalities,
viz. British, Canadian, French, New Zealand, Gurkha, Polish
and Indian troops, plus seventy thousand Italians. In the case
of numbers of men the two sides were equal, but the Allies

were superior in other ways: German guns, 1,300 and tanks eight hundred; Allied guns three thousand and tanks three thousand.

The taking of Rome followed quickly. There was no fighting in the city. The Fifth Army moved in and occupied it for a time. However, the American commander Lieutenant General Mark Clark made a mistake by not chasing up the enemy in enough strength. Too many troops got away to carry on the war. Mark was revelling in the victory.

The Eighth Army was advancing on their front which bypassed Rome. Our unit was now northeast of Rome. I found out that a supply lorry was going to the city. I can't remember how I did it, but I managed to get a lift. It was a wonderful experience, though I had only one and a half hours in Rome. The first place I visited was the Vatican. It is a marvellous building. The statues, marble figures and mosaics are incredible, in number as well as in beauty. I climbed up to the vast balcony which is above the main entrance. Here on the balustrade are figures of the twelve apostles. There were numerous visitors around me and I had to hurry on because there was more to be seen. It was just five days after the liberation. As I walked along from the Vatican to see the King Victor Emmanuel memorial I thought perhaps somebody would show a sign of recognising an English soldier. People seemed to ignore and almost look through me. The memorial is a wonderful building or, say, palace, in white stone, as far as I could see not used for any purpose. It is situated in an open space about a quarter of a mile from the Colosseum, a large part of which is still standing with some of the terraces visible. There were some people being shown round when I arrived there. The guide was speaking in English. I managed to hear him say there used to be a zoo adjoining the site and that lions were brought through an underground passageway to make a meal of the Christian martyrs. I did not stay there very long as I was anxious to get my lift back to camp.

On Saturday 10th June I received a telegram from Mother, saying that my sister Peggy had died on Tuesday 6th June. I was severely shocked. I had always thought she would recover. My lips were sealed for twenty-four hours. To me the loss was devastating. There was no link, but it seems odd that Peggy died on the day of the invasion of Europe.

Now follows a time when the echelon was on the move constantly because of the advance of the troops. It was necessary to get as far forward as possible before winter came. However, we seemed to move in varying directions. One day we arrived at a vineyard. There were many rows of vines well spaced apart. I could not see any buildings about attached to the yard. In a few days we travelled to a village very close to the enemy. It was a mistake. We had been turned away from a country house and grounds. The vehicles were lined up along a secondary road in the village. There were houses and bungalows on either side of the road. Some of the properties were empty. We all moved under cover for evening was approaching. I put my camp bed in the hall of a bungalow which was empty. After midnight the enemy started shelling the village. I expect the guns were mounted on mobile track vehicles. They were moved up under cover of darkness. It was really frightening as I hadn't been under gunfire before. There was no point in it but I kept my head under the blanket – well, it reduced the noise but it wouldn't have stopped any shrapnel. The shelling was sporadic for nearly two hours. Next morning there appeared to be no damage to our vehicles. We moved straight away to a safer place.

On one occasion we settled ourselves into an orchard which was fine. However, the weather changed to a very wet period. The mountain range, the Apennines, caused a lot of rain to fall. Believe me, it can pour torrents in Italy, especially in the autumn. When the time came to move it was a nightmare. The ground became a sea of mud as our three-ton lorries tried to move out though the vehicles had four-wheel drive which helped. However, I thought I might be seasick as I was swayed about so much.

On another day the echelon drew on to a wide-open grassed area. It seemed a good spot. The grass was close-cropped. We all escaped from our vehicles and sat or slept in the sun. Suddenly a loud shout alerted us that something was wrong. I was leaning against the back wheel of the stores lorry. Somebody had seen a big snake curled up on the inside of the front wheel. My blood froze. I was really frightened and mesmerized. I hated reptiles. One of the NCOs brought along his loaded pistol and shot it – what a relief. That evening we slept outside as usual; the weather was good. However, I dug myself a slit trench for my bed. I thought I would be safer from any animal. Also I thought if there were any bombs dropped I might escape injury. There were very few casualties amongst our forward troops. There was one very sad occurrence, however, to one of our sergeants who was a very pleasant man. His troop had moved to a new position and Sergeant Bright had dug himself a slit trench like the other men. In the evening the enemy were sending mortar shells over. The sergeant was in his trench but one of the shells fell right into the middle of his back. As they say, it must have had his name on it. I felt very emotional later when I had to deal with his personal effects.

So far we had been travelling mostly northwards and were approaching Arezzo. Here we turned southeast. The echelon found refuge in a prisoner of war camp, or it may have been a concentration prison. It was empty. There were rough double wooden bunk beds in every room. I came across some quite big nails with the ends filed down to make a blade. Some of the troopers went scavenging around the local area. They came across a farm which was unoccupied. Several chickens were brought, cooked and passed around. What a pleasure to have nice tasty food, although we could have been court-martialled for looting.

Our next move was towards the east coast. I don't know who was doing the map reading but the echelon was heading for

San Marino. San Marino is a very small independent state in Italy. It was neutral. It could have been a very difficult position if we had invaded it. It might have caused an international incident! Every vehicle turned round very smartly. Down the road we came across a brickworks which had ceased production. It proved a very useful stopping place for us. We could sleep under cover amongst all the dust, bricks and tiles.

It was about this time that I was promoted from unpaid Lance Corporal to paid Lance Corporal. I deserved it for all the responsibility I had taken on. It would certainly make a difference to my demobilisation pay.

Eventually the echelon arrived at a seaside town, Cervia, where we were going to spend a good deal of the winter. The big push had now faded out. There were several reasons for this new situation. The Fifth Army on the west side had its strength reduced from 250,000 men to 130,000. There were reductions in the Eighth Army too. The troops were needed for the new front in southern France. In addition, the Germans had received reinforcements. Low-lying land in the approaches to the Po valley was heavy and muddy after very heavy rains. By December 1944 all forward movements had ceased. On hearing this news the Joint Chiefs of Staff had acquired other units to be moved to other duties – some went to Greece.

In Cervia the SQMS and I were inspecting billets for all our troops. It was a busy time. I was allowed a room in a small bungalow. The place was fairly modern. The front room allotted to me was good. The floor had terrazzo tiling and there was plenty of room for all my kit and camp bed. I had the cheek to take in an ammunition box to act as a stove for heating. There was a pipe to take the smoke away. The small window had a sheet of glass which you could slide out. I removed the glass and put the chimney pipe through the space. A sheet of metal held the pipe in position. I burned wooden blocks in the stove which was held off the floor by some bricks. The climate in northern Italy can be very cold in winter, especially on the east side, and I couldn't bear being cold.

There was a café in the town situated in an open area. There was a space by the building that was enclosed by a wooden fence. It was decided that meals would be prepared and served here. A tarpaulin was put over the fenced area to act as a roof. It seemed a rather rough affair. Well, it was only to be a temporary arrangement.

What was really extraordinary was that I met my brother-in-law there. My sister Molly had met and married him at Warminster, our home town. It was like a lot of war-time marriages – it was done in a hurry. I had never met him before so it was strange in a way. I suppose I should have thanked him for looking me up. We became quite well acquainted. However, he was too fond of heavy drinking for my liking. He became friendly with another heavy drinker in the echelon. I did not see much more of him because his regiment was on the move but Tony and I have remained good friends. I regret to say Molly and Tony were divorced some time ago.

As there was no movement forward in the army, men were being sent on leave to different places. I was lucky with three other fellows to get a week's holiday in Florence which was not too far from Cervia. There was a camp for Service personnel. Good sleeping accommodation, food and a NAAFI was all on tap. An Italian dance band played at different times in the leisure hall which produced a good atmosphere. Walking round the city was interesting and fascinating. I was excited when we came across the Opera House where there were two operas being performed that week – *Aida* by Verdi and *Madame Butterfly* by Puccini. I persuaded the fellows with me to go and see *Aida* which came first. We were able to get a box for all of us and the cost appeared reasonable. We arrived at the venue in good time. In the box it was something of a disappointment because the seats were hard-seated cane chairs, but the view of the auditorium and the stage was excellent. The place was packed out. It was a real thrill to hear a full orchestra playing. The curtain was raised and the performance began. The singing was excellent; good voices, but to me there was nobody who was outstanding. I don't think my friends were quite so keen so they didn't want to go on to see *Madame Butterfly*. I had to have a seat in the front stalls for *Butterfly*. It was another lovely evening for me. The house was again full to capacity. Perhaps the opera performances closed down when Italy was invaded. During the interval the bar was very full and what a glittering scene that was.

Back at Cervia it became clear we were moving again, this time to Ravenna. I remember I had to act as commander in an armoured Daimler car that was being driven to Ravenna. It was an order that an armoured car had to have two men on board. It was a bitterly cold day and I was frozen stiff. In Ravenna most of the roads were sheets of ice. The stores were set up in some person's garage. There was no heating there and the floor was of concrete. I was lucky to have my folding bed and at night I piled as many things on top of me as I could to keep warm. It was a hard time, but harder still for men in the front line and facing danger.

In the spring of 1945 the final action was taken. Some German troops had been recalled home for battle elsewhere. There had been replacements, but not of the same strength or quality. Some German defences in the mountains had been physically strengthened. Nevertheless, the German generals were not happy with their situation. They had flooded areas between two rivers as part of their defence. They thought a fighting retreat to the Alps was the best plan, but Hitler would not have approved that idea. The Allied troops had had some increase in manpower and military strength. Many thousands of Italian regular troops made a strong force. Brazil had declared war on the Axis powers in 1942 and now sent a force of 25,000 men to Italy. Also, a British Army Jewish brigade arrived from the Middle East. Most valuable of all were two divisions which arrived from the USA. One was an elite group fully trained in mountain warfare who caused the Germans to receive many casualties.

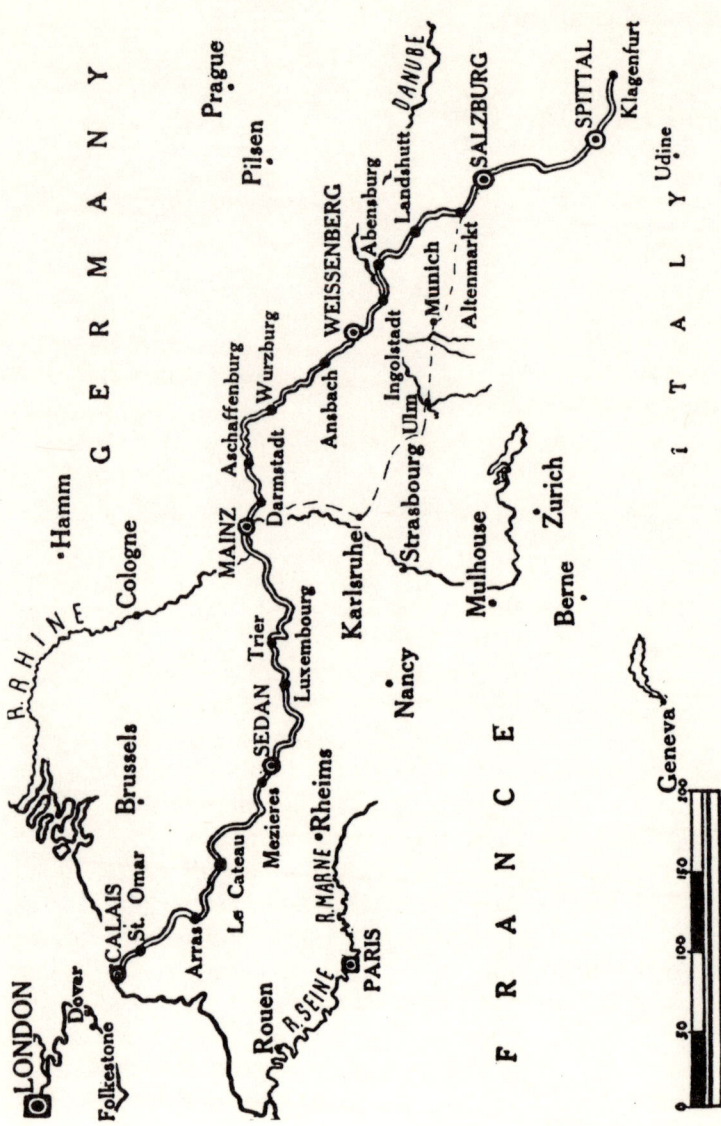

8 · *Winding Up*

Eventually resistance to the 8th Army and the American 5th Army failed. The 12th Royal Lancers had the job of heading round the shores of the Adriatic which was quite hectic. To my disappointment, we didn't go into Venice because it would have held up our momentum. Without too much effort we arrived at Trieste. The squadron set itself up in a suburb of the town. The SQMS and I went into the centre and found the Fascist Headquarters. In the entrance to the building there was a large hall. At the far end there was a soldier standing next to a loaded machine gun which was on a mount. It looked as though it was ready for action. There were a number of British troops wandering through the building, which comprised a large number of offices. I was astounded when the SQMS picked up a typewriter and wrapped a blanket round it. He carried it downstairs through the hall and nobody made any attempt to stop him. Of course, other people were taking other items but nothing so bulky as a typewriter.

The stores and office were set up in a hall of the local school. It was all very nice, the local people were friendly. One of my pals took me into someone's home and we were given a small meal – fried egg, etc but I didn't enjoy it as the egg seemed all dried up. I think it must have been overdone in olive oil.

The sergeants had set themselves up with a sergeants' mess, a place where they had their own meals and social events. The corporals were suddenly imbued with the wish to have their own mess too. However, it failed to materialise.

One day I had the chance to go on leave to Venice; however, I didn't go. I turned it down partly because my pal and I were getting interested in two local girls. I have regretted missing out on that chance ever since.

On 2nd May the Germans signed the surrender agreement at Caserta. The war in Italy had ceased, officially – what a relief.

I took advantage of the fine weather and went for a swim in the Adriatic. The water was beautifully warm. It was 8th May.

The pal I have mentioned was the squadron clerk and we were sharing the same office. The two girls who interested us lived in a cottage high up the hill behind the school where we worked. We met them one evening when we were out for a stroll. They were seated in the front garden of their cottage. My pal started chatting them up as he had learnt some Italian, but I hadn't bothered. I can't remember how many times we visited them. My Italian was improving quite considerably. The dark-haired girl, Ester, could play the piano and one evening we went into the cottage – she played the piano while I sang. Yes, it was getting romantic. I became smitten, but fate was about to take a part in the matter. My father was ill at home, but I did not know how seriously. Major Teichman, a well known retired officer at home, had managed to get me on special leave back· to England. I had no idea about this. I obtained Ester's address before I left – it was Ester Piresi, Strada del Friuli 41, Trieste and I wrote her a letter in very poor Italian while I was in England.

Overland travelling for men of the 8th Army was an excellent idea. It was referred to as LIAP. The men were going home on leave for compassionate reasons. Three-tonner trucks were converted by having a long seat fitted on each side. The roofs were covered with tarpaulins. The front and back were left open. The arrangement was not plush but suitable enough for experienced troops. The journey started from Villach in Austria through Germany, Luxembourg, and France. There were several stops overnight for sleep and refreshments. Two experiences stand out in my mind. At Ulm in Southern Germany I was astounded to see hundreds of houses damaged by bombing. Yet in the middle of it all the cathedral was still standing intact. It has the tallest spire in Europe. The journey through Luxembourg was brief but I was very impressed with the cleanliness, brightness and neatness of the place. Of course, they hadn't been in a war.

It was marvellous arriving in England. There were leave passes and travel warrants to take us to our homes. I had never been so pleased before to get home to Warminster. Mother was delighted to see me. Her life was hard. When Peggy was in Winsley Hospital she had had to be visited once a week, and then came her death and funeral arrangements. Next, Dad had become ill and had been given treatment in Bath Hospital. He was suffering from an enlarged spleen and was too ill to do anything. The family doctor told me he would not recover. The news came as a shock. At home Dad was in a double bed in the main living room. It was easier to have him there than in a bedroom. The gramophone and music business had to be kept going for an income.

It was good to have a drink in the local pub again and do some socialising. When the time came for me to return to Italy Dad was upset and cried. He said there was a livelihood to be made in the shop. I replied thank you, but I did not promise anything.

We returned in the three-tonner lorries again, but not quite by the same route. It was a thrill as we went through the Brenner Pass. However, there was a disappointment on arrival back at the regiment. It had moved away towards Austria. I gave some thought what to do about Ester. It was all so difficult. I didn't really know her; my Italian was poor and there was no way of meeting because transport was not available. How long would it be before I was demobbed? Our backgrounds and religions were so obviously different. These may seem weak

Saturday Night Soldier

excuses to some people, but I am a pragmatic individual. My enthusiasm died. Girls at home were more easily available.

At our new site there was a good place for the stores and office. I had also been able to get a radio for entertainment. One evening I did a reckless thing. I was passing the sergeants' mess and one of them called me into their bar. He had a half pint of cognac. Would I drink it in one go? Being a greedy type and, for once, adventurous, I agreed. Well, I didn't feel anything much at first. I walked back to the office and sat on my bed. Gradually a warm feeling permeated my whole body. There were no ill effects.

Soon the regiment was on the move again. We arrived at Villach in Austria. Here it was a very pleasant location. There was some fraternisation with the Austrians but I had no female attractions. There was a booklet issued to troops to help them in speaking German where the German words were written with phonetic pronunciation with their meaning in English.

In the office I had to teach someone to take over my job. It took quite a while, as not everyone had a sense of responsibility. Accuracy was also a necessary qualification and it was also important to be able to type. It was imperative that the other ranks did not draw more money than they were entitled to have. It was difficult to recover debts. The only way was to stop paying out to that person on pay day.

Time was drawing near for my departure. I had to return to England to a training unit and there wait for the correct time to move. The Squadron Quarter Master Sergeant tried his best to persuade me to sign on as a regular soldier. It came as something of a surprise to me. I thanked him, but I was keen to get back to 'civvy street'. It had much more appeal to me. I had had enough of military life despite the relatively good time it had been with the 12th Royal Lancers.

I shed no tears the day I left the regiment. It was now a series of transit camps awaiting me. Down into Italy was the route. At times it seemed rather dodgy and 'hit and miss', but eventually I reached Milan. The camp was a collecting point for personnel returning to the UK. I had the chance to see the well-known city and I bought some presents for the family at home. There was some excellent architecture to view. However, the best was the cathedral. The building is a wonderful sight. On the other hand, the inside cannot compare with the beauty of the Vatican where the statuary and mosaics are wonderful. The stay there was fairly brief. The journey from Milan was by rail through the Alps. More wonderful scenery was a treat. The line led us round Lake Lausanne. The train slowed down and almost stopped in the station at Lausanne. Suddenly some men jumped on the coach. They were giving out leaflets in English to advertise the beauties and facilities of their country and town. The train moved on fairly rapidly. In the suburbs of Paris I got a glimpse of the Eiffel Tower. We journeyed on to the channel coast and I was on my way back to the 61st Training Regiment RAC at Darlington. From there I was to be demobbed in 1946. However, I was lucky to get a week's leave for Christmas 1945.

I had to return to the regiment after Christmas to await the right date for demobilisation. One evening I went to the cinema that had been built in the regimental grounds. It was a very good size and had excellent equipment. However, it was very strange because I was the only person in the place.

In January I was sent on my journey south to Taunton. Here was one of the demob centres. Here I was issued with a complete suit of clothes, shoes, socks, vests and pants.

Then I was on my way home – the last journey paid for by the army. I often think I had a good war and was lucky to get away without any injury. The experience was invaluable, but over six years of my life had gone for ever.

23564   Army Form X 202/B.

CERTIFICATE OF TRANSFER to the ARMY RESERVE

Army No. ......**556423**...... Rank ....**Tpr**................

Surname (Block letters) ....**SIMINSON**................

Christian Name(s) ....*John Reginald William*.........

Regt. or Corps ...................**R.A.C.**..................

The transfer of the above-named to the appropriate Class of the Army

Reserve (see note below) is confirmed with effect from ......**7.4.46**......*

>   *The date to be inserted here will be that following the day on which
>   Release Leave terminates, including any additional leave to which the
>   soldier may be entitled by virtue of service overseas.

>   Note.—The appropriate Class of the Army Reserve is as follows :—

>   (i) Royal Army Reserve—in the case of a regular soldier with reserve
>   service to complete :

>   (ii) Army Reserve, Class Z (T)—in the case of a man of the
>   Territorial Army, including those called up for service under the
>   National Service Acts :

>   (iii) Army Reserve, Class Z—in the case of all other soldiers not
>   included in (i) or (ii) above.

Record Office Stamp.

[stamp: Cavalry & ... Corps Office, 9 JAN 1946, BARNET HERTS.]

.... DCO

for Officer i/c ..........**R.A.C.**.. Records.

Date ......**Jun 46**......

Warning.—

Any alteration of the particulars given in this certificate may render the
holder liable to prosecution under the Seamen's and Soldiers' False Characters
Act, 1906.

If this certificate is lost or mislaid, no duplicate can be obtained.

Wt. 45088/4735 1000M 2/45 KJL/7396/16 Gp. 38/3.